To Theresa,

Live with
intention !

Lauren
Archer

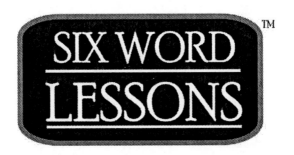

ON CHANGING HABITS

100 Lessons
to
Stop Self-Sabotage
and
Gain Self-Mastery

Lauren Archer, CHT

Lauren-Archer.com

Editing by Patty Pacelli

Published by Pacelli Publishing
9905 Lake Washington Blvd. NE, #D-103
Bellevue, Washington 98004
Pacellipublishing.com

ISBN-10: 1-933750-40-5
ISBN-13: 978-1-933750-40-8

Dedication

To Laila and Ethan

*As you listen to your heart
and connect with your inner wisdom,
you can accomplish virtually anything
you set your mind to.*

May you live the life of your dreams.

Acknowledgements

Thank you for choosing to explore the ideas in this book. These lessons are a compilation of tips, tricks, and best practices I have gathered over thirty-plus years of study and practice as a student of consciousness, health coach and hypnotherapist.

I offer deep respect and appreciation to the many, many teachers and authors who have influenced me with their insights, and who have led by example. I'm grateful to my clients who have opened their hearts and minds as they shared their struggles, stories, and successes. I've been blessed to have experienced my share of personal obstacles and challenges which have humbled, stretched and strengthened me, and deepened my capacity to empathize with others' struggles in changing habits.

My writing has benefited from the influence of my beloved life partner, Kristjan, an avid chess player and deep thinker with uncanny insight into human behavior. I am grateful beyond words for Kris's love, generosity of spirit, encouragement, support, and editorial prowess.

Last but not least, I want to thank the amazing women of Eastside Women in Business, especially Patty Pacelli, for encouraging me to put pen to paper so I can share these ideas as elegantly as possible within the succinct format of a Six-Word Lessons Book.

Introduction

"Sow a thought, and you reap an act;
Sow an act, and you reap a habit;
Sow a habit, and you reap a character;
Sow a character, and you reap a destiny."
— Samuel Smiles

Your life is a culmination of the sum total of your habits. The small individual choices you make on a daily basis add up to incrementally influence your life, in either productive or unproductive ways.

Many people have fallen into their predominant lifestyle habits by default, with little conscious direction or forethought. With few exceptions, habits are *learned* behaviors (from family, society, or subculture), and therefore can be unlearned and relearned. Whether or not the learning process is easy or difficult depends on *how you choose to think about* your habits.

I'm somewhat of an expert in habit change, having successfully shifted many of my own stubborn patterns personally, as well as helping thousands of people transform their lives in my private practice. As a student of consciousness, my studies have revealed some very efficient, effective strategies that can make the process of habit change seem nothing short of miraculous.

> *"I have been battling an addiction problem for years with little to no success until I went to see Lauren. After my visit with her I followed her instructions to the letter and have never looked back. Lauren gave me my life back*

and I have been addiction-free from that day to the present. I owe her everything. Thank you so much Lauren, you are the best!" -- Rosanna S., Everett, WA

"What started off as a last ditch effort to quit smoking has turned into so much more. I hadn't imagined how much of an impact my mind was having on my daily actions and my potential for greatness. You are truly a 'chiropractor of the mind.' I value how you are able to quickly dissect my reasoning and effectively change my train of thought and view of things. Thank you for helping me out of some old ruts of life and helping me realize how to use my mind to capitalize on life and improve my business." -- Mike P., Kirkland, WA

My wish for you is that within the lessons of this book you discover the keys that unlock the power of your mind so that you can live your life more fully and freely, releasing the habits that have held you back, and creating purposeful habits that empower you to be your very best.

To learn more about a private session, please visit:

Lauren-Archer.com

How to Use This Book

You can use these lessons to help you **effectively end a problem habit** (like smoking, overeating, drugs or alcohol, procrastination, negative thinking, etc.). You can also use this book to **firmly establish a new habit** (like exercising, eating healthfully, enjoying sobriety, taking productive action, thinking positively).

Changing your habits consciously leads to self-mastery. As you explore the following lessons, don't underestimate their power. These timeless principles are elegantly simple yet extraordinarily effective. Remember that when one door closes, another one opens. Let's cross your new threshold now, as you choose to live your life on purpose.

Table of Contents

A Change of Mind Changes Everything

1

Prime your mind for optimal results.

Throughout this book, you are priming your consciousness with positive tools and strategies to make healthy changes. Give your mind the important position it deserves in your life. Your predominant thoughts and feelings influence every decision you make. Start paying attention to your inner world in order to maximize this valuable resource

2

Begin with positive outcomes in mind.

Before you embark on your journey to healthier habits, be sure to invest some time and energy to conjure up as many positive images as you can of how wonderful you'll feel once your chosen habit pattern is well established. Refer to these images often. Imagine yourself saying, "That was easier than I thought it would be."

3

Be willing to adjust your beliefs.

As Einstein said, "Problems cannot be solved with the same mindset that created them." Have the willingness to accept that some of your beliefs may need a minor adjustment, perhaps even a radical change. Get curious as you investigate your current beliefs about yourself and your relationship to the world around you as you explore new possibilities.

4

Become aware of awareness with mindfulness.

You can't change what you're not aware of. Act as if you are a third party observer. Monitor your mind's activities as an impartial witness. Pay attention to your attention. Notice what you notice. Listen to your inner dialogue. Observe your observations. Release judgment and criticism. Simply notice impartially what's going on in your mind.

5

Distinguish your servant from your master.

The mind is a wonderful servant but a terrible master. Remember that you are the master, and your mind is your servant. If your mind has been acting like an untrained puppy that is pulling you in all directions, it's time to implement a mental obedience training program by applying the principles in this book.

6

Question your fundamental premises and conclusions.

False premises lead to faulty conclusions. Become aware of premises like, "I need something external to make me feel better," or "I always fail at this," or "I'm stressed so all bets are off." Instead, you can ask yourself clarifying questions like, "Is this really true?" or, "Will my chosen action give me the results I really want, or merely what I think I want?"

7

Separate yourself from your problem habit.

You are not your behavior. Take an objective look at the situation. Avoid moral judgments. Resist defining your habits as good vs. bad, or right vs. wrong. Instead, analyze whether your habits are productive or unproductive, functional or dysfunctional, helpful or harmful. When you release negative judgments, you free up energy to make lasting change.

Know What You are Dealing With

8

Clearly define your objectives and reasons.

What do you want and why do you want it? If your objectives are vague and your reasons are superficial, you're likely to give up from lack of energy. Having clearly defined objectives along with significant, meaningful reasons will provide the spark of enthusiasm and sustainable "oomph" you need to persevere through the inevitable challenges of life.

9

Use questions appropriately for positive change.

The quality of the questions you ask determines the quality of the results you get. Don't ask, "Why me?" or, "Why can't I ever do this right?" Instead, ask, "How can I perceive this differently?" "Where are the opportunities in this situation?" "What else can I do to feel good?" Program your mind to seek productive answers.

10

Be blatantly honest with yourself.

Ignoring, hiding, or avoiding the truth keeps you trapped in a cycle of denial. When you acknowledge the truth, no matter how uncomfortable it may be, you empower yourself to change. Telling the truth (to yourself and others) strengthens your integrity and lets you make decisions with facts, not fiction. Now is the time to get real.

11

Acceptance is a prerequisite for change.

Navigating from point A to point B requires setting a course of action from where you are. Accept your current location without defending, explaining or justifying how you got there. Establish where you are now as your starting point (even if it's not where you want to be), so you can begin heading towards your destination.

12

Acknowledge, honor and release the past.

The past may have shaped you, but it does not define you. You can transform traumas, disappointments, abuse, or challenging circumstances by choosing to forgive and rise above. Holding feelings of anger or resentment, or feeling like a victim or martyr limits your ability to grow. Bless and release your past and start living from this moment forward.

13

Stop the blame game for good.

Take responsibility for the choices you make, regardless of your outer circumstances. Other people's negative attitudes or opinions are not an excuse for overindulgence of unproductive behaviors. As author Richard Bach says, "Argue for your limitations, and sure enough, they're yours." If you hear yourself placing blame or making an excuse, immediately stop and focus on your desired outcome.

14

Understand what habitual behavior really is.

A habit is a simply a learned behavior pattern, stored as long term muscle memory in the subconscious mind, so that the behavior can be performed almost automatically, without conscious effort. Habits are essential to daily functioning. They free up your conscious mind to think of other things, and are your brain's "go-to" responses in times of stress.

15

Recognize what habitual behavior is NOT.

Habitual behavior is definitely not a symptom of an inherent character flaw, nor suggestive of any personality "type." If you've struggled to overcome a habit and haven't succeeded so far, this doesn't mean you're weak-willed or incapable of change. Whatever habitual behavior you have learned, you CAN unlearn and relearn another.

16

Habit vs addiction: Know the difference.

The line between habit and addiction is a fine one. While habits are automatic behaviors created by repetition, they slide into addictions when you feel a compulsion or need for a certain substance or behavior. Even though professional help may be required for certain addictions, the principles in this book build a positive foundation to create lasting changes.

17

There's no such thing as self–sabotage.

As radical as this may sound, blaming self-sabotage for unproductive behavior is a misperception of the truth. Saying "I sabotage myself" usually means that you have two or more inner aspects that are in conflict. If one part of you wants to stop or start a new habit, and another part of you is resisting, you'll continue to struggle until you create an internal peace treaty.

18

Make a peace treaty with yourself.

We all just want to feel good. Behind every behavior is an inner aspect of you that has a positive intention (usually to feel better, safer, more protected, or more accepted in some way). Even your "inner critic" wants you to succeed. Seek to acknowledge and fulfill that positive intention in healthy ways to release inner conflict and experience more peace.

Prepare Your Environment for Optimal Results

19

Identify the resources you already have.

Whether it's a good supportive friend, a character trait like perseverance or resilience, or even a minor degree of control over your environment, make a list of all possible resources that can support you during the change process. Like training wheels on a new bicycle, your resources will help stabilize you during the learning phase.

20

Create your "habit-change care package."

Make change as easy as possible by gathering additional resources that can help you succeed. Stock your home or office with healthy replacement items (like gum or mints, non-alcoholic beverages, approved snacks). Gather necessary equipment and information (i.e., have your gym bag ready, walking shoes by the door, lists of action items visible).

21

Prepare yourself by removing unhealthy temptations.

Out of sight, out of mind is a healthy rule of thumb. Eliminate temptations from your environment to the best of your ability, and refuse to let them back into your home, office, or life. If others in your life indulge, ask them to help you. Let them know you prefer to keep temptations out of sight.

22

Set visual reminders in your environment.

What you see in your environment influences your state of mind. Hide the cooking magazines and replace them with fitness magazines. Make a "Vision Board" with images that remind you of your desired outcome. Put notes or symbols on your bathroom mirror, on your refrigerator, and on your computer. Keep your goal fresh in your mind.

23

Keep a list of positive affirmations.

What you say to yourself (and how you say it) profoundly influences your experience. Be especially selective about those words that follow the phrase, "I am." Tell yourself "I am capable, I can do this." Or you may choose to say "even though I haven't yet reached my goal, I am making progress and strengthening my resolve."

24

Empower your thoughts with guided visualization.

Listen to guided imagery audio programs to activate the power of your subconscious mind. You'll get to mentally rehearse your new habit and imagine receiving the benefits. Soothing musical sounds and reassuring words can help you relax and focus at a very deep level. Explore my self-help audio guided imagery programs at Lauren-Archer.com.

25

Habits are not broken, they're replaced.

You are not simply stopping one behavior, you are starting another. If you're NOT smoking, drinking alcohol, overeating, gambling, procrastinating, etc., what are you doing instead? Will you be sitting quietly, hands in your lap? Perhaps chewing gum, drinking tea, or attending a class? It's essential to clearly define how you choose to replace your unproductive habit.

26

Choose two or more replacement habits.

The brain likes choices. Provide yourself with a minimum of two, and ideally a longer list of several replacement behaviors that you can easily select as a substitute for your old behavior. For example, if going for a walk is one choice, have several alternative plans in place in case the weather prohibits your best intentions.

Success Leaves Clues.
Start Reading Them.

27

Model someone who is already successful.

Find someone who has already established the kind of habits you would like to add to your life (someone you know, or simply know of) and use their example as inspiration. What you admire in others, you actually strengthen in yourself. Seek to discover how they think, act, and believe. Imitate their behavior patterns until they become your own.

28

Be willing to ask for help.

Dare to enlist the help of a mentor or coach. Seeking support is a healthy sign of strength, intelligence, and maturity. Successful people are usually willing to offer a helping hand to those who want to follow in their footsteps. Remember that asking politely for what you want greatly enhances your probability of getting it.

29

Nourish and cultivate your inner virtues.

Do you have a lack of patience? Weak motivation? No determination? You're in luck. You can consciously nurture the growth of specific virtues within yourself to help you establish your new habit. Close your eyes and imagine planting seeds of determination in the fertile soil of your mind. Give that virtue the nourishment of your care and attention and let it grow.

30

Inspire yourself with others' success stories.

This is especially important if you've unsuccessfully tried to change your habits in the past. It's tempting to give up hope when things get tough. Lots of ordinary people break through limitations and accomplish deep and meaningful change every day. Thanks to the internet, you can search for stories of people like you who have made lasting change.

31

Partner with a friend for accountability.

Select someone who cares enough to hold you accountable for your actions. Make a verbal or written agreement that you will follow through on your chosen habit, and schedule regular days and times to communicate and report your progress. Being accountable to another human being helps many people stay dedicated, motivated, and on track.

32

Create a mental prototype for success.

What are the primary archetypal qualities of the kind of person you would like to become? A strong hero? A mighty champion? A compassionate healer? A feisty comedian? A brilliant inventor? A poised professional? A rock star? An enlightened master? Use your imagination and let those powerful archetypal qualities come to life within you.

33

What you learned you can unlearn.

At the core level, all habits are learned behaviors. Let's not overcomplicate the change process with complex excuses or fears of inadequacy. Keep it simple. You have learned millions of behaviors over your lifetime, like brushing your teeth or tying your shoes. Habit change is ultimately about learning. Remember that your capacity to learn is alive and well.

34

Fake it until you make it.

One of the most powerful tools for personal growth, "Act as if," is a simple and profound principle that can make the change process easier than you may imagine. Literally pretend that you've already made the change. Your brain doesn't know the difference between a real experience and an imagined experience, so imagine that you've already transformed.

35

Choose to stand for, not against.

As Wayne Dyer wisely pointed out, "Everything you are against weakens you. Everything you are for strengthens you." Define what you are standing for, who you are becoming, and what direction you are heading. When you turn away from your old habit, what are you turning toward? What positive principles are you standing for with your new behavior?

36

Give life itself credit for synchronicity.

We live in an interconnected, intelligent universe. You participate in and influence your experience of reality, but you are not solely responsible for creating it. When you align your thoughts, words, and actions, you may discover what others have: a sense of being in the flow of life, with an increase in happy surprises, meaningful coincidences, and synchronistic opportunities.

Continue as Long as it Takes

37

Expect a brief awkward learning phase.

Mastery is not automatic. In order to get comfortable with a new behavior, you may first have to navigate through an "in-between" time, where your old habit hasn't yet been eliminated and your new habit isn't yet established. Don't mistake the awkward feelings as a sign that things aren't working. This is a natural phase of the process.

38

Inch by inch, life's a cinch.

The old saying is true: Inch by inch, life's a cinch, yard by yard, life is hard. Avoid getting overwhelmed by trying to do too much, too soon. If you're feeling daunted, bring your attention to the present moment, and focus on the single hour and day at hand. Don't "future trip." Simply do what's in front of you to do.

39

Identify the smallest possible action step.

Break your large objective into incremental components and start small. Whether it's removing a substance from your home, putting your sneakers by the door, or scheduling an event on your calendar, find one positive action step and get started. Taking initiative sets a proactive pattern in motion which reverses the cycle of inertia and negativity.

40

Take one forward step each day.

Even if it's a minuscule step, performing at least one small task each day keeps your momentum heading in the direction of your dreams. The consistency of your actions reinforces your intent. Incremental actions repeated over time create a substantial cumulative effect. This also tells your brain you mean business and establishes credibility in your consciousness.

41

"Leap frog" over resistance and obstacles.

In the children's game of Leap Frog, one child propels over another squatting child and lands on the other side. Use your imagination to "leap" over short term discomfort (like exercising, or saying no to unhealthy choices). Let your mind "land" on all the good feelings you will experience once you have followed through on your new habit.

42

Where your attention goes, energy flows.

Don't allow yourself to ruminate on what you can't have or what's missing in your life, because what you focus on, you get more of. Redirect your attention to what you CAN do, what you CAN have, and what is going RIGHT for you. Think of your attention as being like a flashlight beam that you can aim. Shine it on your desired outcome.

43

Set a timer to limit exposure.

Let's face it--there are days when your motivation levels are higher than others. When you don't feel like doing something you promised yourself you'd do, set a timer for a short time period (about ten to twenty minutes) and do what you can during that time frame. This valuable process helps you to keep your word and strengthen your resolve.

44

Things get easier as time passes.

Keep this in mind when you feel the pull of the past: the farther away from the edge of the cliff you walk, the easier it is not to backslide down the slippery slope. As you leave your old habit behind, each step you take in the opposite direction fortifies your ability to continue forward on your path of success.

45

Repetition must often be repeated repeatedly.

Some say it takes 21 days for a behavior to become habit, but research indicates that's only the beginning. Depending on how deeply embedded your previous habit was, it may take hundreds of iterations for your new habit to fully replace the old. Keep repeating your new behavior pattern over and over, knowing that each iteration deepens your learning.

46

Anticipating future rewards will enhance wellbeing.

Research reveals that optimistically looking forward to a positive experience has virtually the same (if not better) beneficial physiological responses as the experience itself. Having something pleasant to look forward to gives you a reason to get up in the morning and persevere. Keep yourself motivated by strategically placing opportunities for rewards in your future.

47

Delayed gratification blows instant gratification away.

It's worth remembering that the sense of personal gratification you gain after having earned something and waited patiently for it far exceeds that of having it handed to you instantly. You are earning your success one positive action at a time. Be patient with the process, and savor the time in between as you await your reward.

48

Give your future self a gift.

If you don't feel like doing it now, you probably won't want to do it later either, so get it over with and do it now as a gift to your future self. Imagine a future version of yourself looking back at the actions you took today, thanking you for your efforts so that you can reap the rewards.

Master the Art of Mental Association

49

Decide to rewire your mental associations.

Your brain is associative by nature, containing a complex network of connections for pleasure or pain, comfort or discomfort, ease or effort. While seemingly fixed, these associations are in fact malleable and subject to repatterning. Contrary to popular belief, your preferences are not etched in stone. You can DECIDE to like what's good for you.

50

"Unaquire" your taste for bad habits.

Because you can acquire a taste, it stands to reason that you can also unacquire a taste. When you don't want something in the first place, you won't feel deprived by leaving it behind. You can consciously choose to dislike habits that no longer serve you by focusing on what you don't like about the behavior.

51

Apply negativity for a positive purpose.

Amplify your feelings of disgust and discomfort for the substance or behavior you are leaving behind. Consciously associate the foulest, most repulsive images, sounds, smells and feelings with your old habit. Make it so gross in your mind that you wouldn't even think about repeating that behavior. This process powerfully rewires your mental associations.

52

A craving is only a thought.

Put cravings in their proper perspective. A craving is merely an illusion, a passing fancy, a simple synapse firing in your brain. Don't give cravings any more significance than they deserve. Train your brain to translate cravings as merely electrical impulses to be dismissed, and remember that they generally fade over time.

53

Acquire a taste for healthy habits.

Consciously choose to fully enjoy and appreciate the things that are good for you. Make the decision to focus your mind on every noticeable good thing about your new chosen habit. You can acquire tastes for healthier foods, for exercise, for drinking water, or chewing gum. You can even acquire a taste for silence, stillness, and serenity.

54

Amplify feelings of appreciation and gratitude.

What you appreciate grows in value. As you start acquiring new tastes, pay attention to what you appreciate about your new lifestyle. Notice how it feels in your body to be grateful. Turn up the volume on these feelings, as if you can make them louder, stronger, brighter and clearer. You're creating positive mental associations with healthy habits.

55

Adjust interpretations of meaning and significance.

Generally speaking, nothing has more meaning than what you give it. The level of importance you assign to your actions and behaviors is subject to interpretation, and can vary based on your perception. Choose to perceive the habit you're leaving behind as dull, ambivalent and insignificant. Make your new habit big, bright, meaningful and significant.

56

Put old habits behind a firewall.

Imagine placing a habit you want to eliminate behind a firewall and locking the door. Even if you wanted to repeat that behavior, it's now officially "not an option." Once you've closed that door, you can move on and explore other healthier options. Telling yourself "it's not an option" frees up a tremendous amount of mental energy.

57

The only way out is through.

Now that your old behavior is not an option, you have little choice but to persevere through thick or thin. Rise up to the challenge and push through. As Winston Churchill said, "If you're going through hell, keep going." Don't turn back. There's a light at the end of the tunnel, even if you can't see it.

58

Perceive effort as play, not work.

When you think of changing habits as being a chore, drudgery, or hard work, you impose unnecessary negativity into your experience. Yes, change requires effort to varying degrees, but most people find that when they really want something, the effort required to obtain it is joyful. Get your game on and enjoy the challenge.

59

Use muscle memory to your advantage.

When you learn, your brain sends signals through your nervous system, registering the information within every cell in your body. Memorize how it physically feels to follow through on your new habit. Then, on those "off days" when you "just don't feel like" doing what you should, activate your muscle memory and just do it.

60

Notice what makes you feel contracted.

How does your body respond to worry, doubt, fear or resentment? Perhaps you shrink back, slump down, or pull away? Your chest contracts, your breathing gets shallow, your heart beats irregularly, and you may sense a knot in the pit of your stomach. Your internal guidance system is giving you important information that something isn't right. Listen.

61

Notice what makes you feel expanded.

How does your body respond to gratitude, appreciation, relief, joy, or love? Perhaps you lean in, rise up, smile, or sigh? Your chest expands, your breathing deepens, and you feel comfortably relaxed and enthusiastic. You may walk with a little extra spring in your step. This is a clue that you're heading in a positive direction.

Develop Inner Strength as You Go

62

Your spoken word is your law.

Do what you say you are going to do. Your spoken promises are meaningless when your words and actions don't coincide. Start by keeping small, simple commitments to yourself. Live with integrity. This means, DON'T say it if you're not fully committed to doing it. If you DO say you're going to do it, be sure to follow through.

63

Be a hero, not a victim.

Create a "complaint-free zone." Rewrite the role you play in the story of your life. Cast yourself as the hero or heroine of your journey, triumphantly victorious over petty complaints, base desires, and presumed entitlements. As Lao Tzu wisely said in the 16th century BCE, "Mastering others is strength, mastering yourself is true power."

64

Strengthen your will with easy tasks.

Find a light task that you can easily perform every day to develop self-discipline. This can be as simple as opening the window blinds, taking a vitamin, moving an object from one side of the shelf to another. The task itself is not important. The value is in the inner strength you gain by following through on your decision.

65

Define your core beliefs and values.

People will jump through nearly any hoop to obtain what they truly value at a deep level. Examine your heart's desires, admit what you truly believe, and give yourself permission to discover what is truly meaningful and important to you. Regardless of what other people say you "should" value, this is your life and it is your responsibility to honor your top priorities.

66

Align your actions with your values.

When your actions are in conflict with your values, you experience internal tension and stress, which weakens your system. The solution is to walk your talk, to live in alignment with your true sense of meaning and purpose. This builds harmony and strength because your thoughts, words, and actions are all focused in the same direction.

67

Give your mind a firm command.

Your mind is like a search engine. It will seek, scan, analyze and optimize whatever you have programmed it to find. If you program it to find what's wrong with life, it will. Firmly command your mind to seek out reasons that you can succeed, why you will succeed, and why you deserve to succeed. Your mind will find those reasons.

68

Keep the best, ditch the rest.

Eliminate the non-essentials that distract you from your goals. Human beings actually *need* very little (water, shelter, food and oxygen). All the rest are *wants*. Avoid accumulating physical, mental, and emotional clutter by separating your needs from your wants. Clear everything out of the way to make room for your new habit to have a place in your life.

69

Reawaken a childlike sense of wonder.

Stretch your mind to see beyond ordinary limitations or the boring, mundane aspects of life. Seek to rediscover simple pleasures. Remember that it's OK not to know all the answers. Marvel at the way your consciousness learns and evolves. You never know what's going to happen next. Stay curious and hopeful.

70

Release attachment to one specific outcome.

Set your internal compass in the direction of your ideal life, and then do what's before you to do. The storms of life will sometimes blow you off course, so be willing to adjust your plans. Resist getting emotionally attached to a particular outcome. Be flexible, stay calm, and keep moving in the direction you believe to be forward.

Handle Setbacks with Grace and Poise

71

Be patient with the change process.

In this age of instant results, it's understandable to get frustrated when change doesn't happen as quickly and as easily as you'd like. Remember that most habits take an initial period of 21 days to take root, followed by six weeks to become established, three months to become second nature, and a full year to become a way of life.

72

There's no such thing as failure.

Replace the word "failure" with "results." Thomas Edison said, "I have not failed. I've just found 10,000 ways that won't work." You can't fail if you keep learning. You may get a different result than you intended, but you can choose to change your approach, acknowledge your efforts, and create a different result next time.

73

Question your motives, examine the consequences.

When you feel pulled toward a particular habit (whether an action or a way of thinking), question your motivation. Why do you want what you want? What are the consequences of having it? What are the consequences of letting it go? Ask yourself, "is this what I REALLY want, or is this what I THINK I want?"

74

Sometimes abstinence is easier than moderation.

For some people, having one bite, one sip, one puff, or one of anything is acceptable. For others, and you know who you are, one leads to two, four, eight, and a bumpy ride down the slippery slope of disaster. This is not a character flaw – it's just a fact of life. Know yourself.

75

Learn to be comfortable being uncomfortable.

Many unproductive habits are a result of earnest attempts to escape feelings of discomfort or stress. Instead, stop resisting and slow down enough to really feel your feelings and listen to your inner guidance. You'll gain much-needed insight, allowing you to transcend and transform naturally. Being comfortable being uncomfortable is a paradoxical state worth mastering.

76

Still a challenge? Change your associations.

If you're feeling stuck, take another look at your mental associations. Do you still have desirable thoughts and feelings for a habit you want to let go of? If so, go back and repeat lessons 50 and 51 with even more emphasis. Do you still have undesirable associations relating to your new habit? Repeat lessons 53 and 54.

77

Forgive yourself for mistakes and mishaps.

The last thing you want to do when you have a setback is beat yourself up with criticism and shame. If you fall back (as many people do), observe your behavior like a curious witness. Notice your triggers. Go back to your mental drawing board and make necessary adjustments. Pat yourself on the back for your willingness to persevere.

78

Take yourself lightly, take life sincerely.

We are all fabulously flawed, perfectly imperfect human beings. Honor your desire to change, keeping in mind that the lessons you are learning along the way are shaping your character. Your sincerity to grow makes a valuable contribution to life itself, and you may be surprised at the way life rewards you with unexpected payoffs for your efforts.

79

Give up needing to be right.

There may be hundreds of justifiable reasons for you to engage in unproductive behavior patterns. Let them go. Life isn't always fair. So be it. Other people can be annoying. Let them. Don't engage in arguments or try to prove your point. Quietly focus on mastering your own behavior, with a humble willingness to learn something in the process.

80

Seek the blessing within the "curse."

Train your brain to get curious during times of disappointment, delay, annoyance or frustration. Ask yourself the question, "Where's the blessing in this?" With this simple query, you program your mind to use challenges for your ultimate benefit. You will naturally gain self-mastery, and will be "on alert" to uncover potential opportunities you may have otherwise missed.

81

Make friends with your inner critic.

Do you experience a nagging inner voice berating your imperfections? Let's assume for a moment that your inner critic wants what you want and it's afraid that if it quiets down, you'll end up homeless or in jail. Acknowledge and thank your inner critic for its good intentions, reassure it that you're in charge, and then give it a much-needed (and welcomed) leave of absence.

Make Your Wellbeing a Top Priority

82

Take action to reduce daily stress.

Honor your need to relieve stress and renew your energy. Take three long, slow, deep breaths. Listen to beautiful music. Infuse your home or office with an uplifting fragrance. Get outside for a 20-minute walk. Read something inspirational. Sit down, relax, close your eyes, and imagine stress melting or evaporating away from your body.

83

Have a "go-to" feel good strategy.

Give yourself permission to do something kind for yourself for at least fifteen minutes every day (as long as it's healthy and in alignment with your goals). Define one or more specific actions you can take that help you feel fabulous. Choose from the previous tip, or get creative. When life gets "wonky," activate your "feel good" strategy.

84

Be patient and compassionate with yourself.

The habit change process is simple, though not always easy. Some people set their minds to make a change and follow through with apparent ease. Others go back and forth with their habit like a bad relationship that drags on for years. Even if you struggle, your sincere desire for change means that you can, and will.

85

Congratulate yourself for every positive step.

Give yourself regular pats on the back. Tell yourself, "great job! I'm doing it! That was easier than I thought!" Focus on progress, not perfection. Reassure yourself that you're heading in the right direction. Take time to appreciate your efforts. You are forging new ground, exploring new territory, learning new behaviors, and building new skills. Bravo!

86

Establish clear, firm, healthy personal boundaries.

As the old saying goes, "Good fences make good neighbors." Like drawing a boundary line, define your own personal behavior boundary line – on one side is what you will do, on the other side is what you will not do. Clarify your position in your own mind, and don't allow others to persuade you to cross your line.

87

Gather courage to "leave your tribe."

When you change a behavior that everyone else in your family, community, or social circle still engages in, you might experience some push-back. Even when you maintain your relationship, in a small but meaningful way you are "leaving your tribe" behind when you disengage from community behaviors. This requires courage, compassion, and a vision of a new tribe.

88

Align yourself with a new "tribe."

Having a sense of belonging is primal to the human psyche. Once you've left your old tribe, align yourself with a new one, even if it's virtual. Whether or not you meet in person, find others who have left unproductive habits behind and who value healthy habits like yours. A supportive community positively influences your ability to succeed.

89

Ships come in over calm seas.

Practice serenity. It's vital to release inner turbulence caused by anger, resentment, worry and fear because these emotions lead to disorganized thinking. Physiologically, negativity manifests with a chaotic heart rate, knots in the pit of your stomach, a weakened immune system, and excess cortisol in the blood stream. When facing inner storms, say "Release, release, release."

Become the Best Version of You

90

From now on, act as if.

Act as if you are happy, successful, relieved, grateful, appreciative, confident, enthusiastic and relaxed. As you act the part, your brain sends electrical impulses to every nerve and muscle fiber in your body. Each time you act as if, your body "learns" the energetic pattern of those states of being. Simply become who you choose to be.

91

Enjoy the feeling of developing character.

Changing habits is one of the best ways to learn about yourself, examine your motives, strengthen your resolve, and grow from within. You may find yourself evolving in ways that you hadn't expected at all as a result of your decision to change. The skills you are developing can be applied in various aspects of life. Celebrate this opportunity.

92

Appreciate the strength of your position.

An old chess axiom instructs students to "play to your strengths." To do this, the pupil must consciously identify strengths (and weaknesses, because every position has some of both). As you appreciate the upside of what could be viewed as difficult, you have successfully identified the strength of your current position and can harness its power.

93

You are becoming a new person.

The process of habit change allows you to more clearly define who you are, what you want, and how you choose to behave. From now on, you are the kind of person who _____ (fill in the blank with your chosen new habit). People who are successful at adopting new behaviors transform all the way through to their core.

94

Repeat after me: Be, do, have.

Some people say "When I have X, I can do Y, then I'll be happy." Instead, reverse the process. This requires a mental leap of faith. Choose to first BE who you want to become, then begin to DO, taking action toward your goals, and then over time, you will HAVE the life you desire.

95

Put the past
far behind you.

Start saying what you will say to yourself once you've left your old habit in the proverbial dust. For example, "I can hardly believe I used to do that! Wow! I'm so glad I don't do THAT anymore. What a relief that phase of my life has shifted! It seems like that was another lifetime ago!"

96

Learn to feel satisfied from within.

Cultivate a physical sense of inner peace, satisfaction and fulfillment. Breathe a sigh of relief and notice how it feels in your system when you reach a state of "enoughness." Remember there is very little outside of yourself that you need. You have nearly everything you need within you. Choose to rest and reflect upon feelings of satisfaction.

97

Dare to live up to life.

Life has issued you a challenge. Accept it. Developing purposeful habits requires vision, courage and persistence. Take the risk. The process of changing habits may not be easy, but it doesn't have to be hard. Dare to step beyond your comfort zone, face your fears, and master your habits once and for all. The results you will experience are well worth your efforts.

98

Engage your heart in your activities.

Live wholeheartedly to the best of your ability. When making daily decisions, notice the sincere inclinations of your heart, and include them in your evaluation process. When your choices are honest and heartfelt, following through is natural because it's the right thing to do, even in those occasions when it's not the easiest thing to do.

99

Give thanks in advance of receiving.

Many people naturally experience gratitude after they have received something they desire. Instead, be grateful even before your goal is fully realized, as an affirmation that the change you desire already exists on some level, even if you can't see or touch it right now. Gratitude is essential to gaining and maintaining good and lasting change.

100

Repeat these lessons for best results.

Repetitions are the way muscle is built. You are building your "habit-change muscle" into one of conscious power through continually incorporating these principles into your life. Remember, if you aren't taking charge of your daily habits, your habits are taking charge of you. From now on, take charge of your life, one habit at a time.

Epilogue

Your success is not an isolated event. I believe that as you set your intention and take positive action toward changing your habits, you send invisible ripples of energy through the quantum field of time and space. Your decision to gain mastery adds substance to the possibility that more of us can make changes for the better. With every success you experience, you benefit each one of us in subtle and meaningful ways. You may become a shining example for others like you who aspire to live more purposefully.

I welcome the opportunity to support you in your journey of transformation.

About the *Six-Word Lessons Series*

Legend has it that Ernest Hemingway was challenged to write a story using only six words. He responded with the story, "For sale: baby shoes, never worn." The story tickles the imagination. Why were the shoes never worn? The answers are left up to the reader's imagination.

This style of writing has a number of aliases: postcard fiction, flash fiction, and micro fiction. Lonnie Pacelli was introduced to this concept in 2009 by a friend, and started thinking about how this extreme brevity could apply to today's communication culture of text messages, tweets and Facebook posts. He wrote the first book, *Six-Word Lessons for Project Managers*, then started helping other authors write and publish their own books in the series.

The books all have six-word chapters with six-word lesson titles, each followed by a one-page description. They can be written by entrepreneurs who want to promote their businesses, or anyone with a message to share.

See the entire *Six-Word Lessons Series* at 6wordlessons.com

For more information on changing habits, go to Lauren-Archer.com